SOUND *Artistry*
INTERMEDIATE METHOD
for CLARINET

PETER BOONSHAFT & CHRIS BERNOTAS

in collaboration with

DR. MARGARET DONAGHUE

T0025116

Thank you for making *Sound Artistry Intermediate Method for Clarinet* a part of your continued development as a musician. This book will help you progress toward becoming a more able and independent musician, focusing on both your technical and musical abilities. It offers material ranging from intermediate to advanced, making it valuable for musicians at various experience levels.

The many instrument-specific exercises in this book will help to support your personal improvement of techniques on your instrument, focusing on skills that may not always be addressed in an ensemble or in other repertoire. You will notice there are many performance and technique suggestions throughout the book. This wonderful advice has been provided by our renowned collaborative partners, as well as the many specialist teachers we worked with to create this book.

Sound Artistry Intermediate Method for Clarinet is organized into lessons that can be followed sequentially. As you progress through each lesson, it is a good idea to go back to previous lessons to reinforce concepts and skills, or just to enjoy performing the music. Exercises include Long Tones, Flexibility, Major and Minor Scales (all forms), Scale Studies, Arpeggio Studies, Chromatic Studies, Etudes, and Duets, as well as exercises that are focused on skills that are particular to your instrument. You will notice that many studies are clearly marked with dynamics, articulations, style, and tempo for you to practice those aspects of performance. Other studies are intentionally left for you to determine those aspects of your musical interpretation and performance. This book progresses through various meters and every key. Once a key has been introduced, previous keys are interspersed throughout for reinforcement and variety. In the back of this book you will also find expanded-range scale pages and a detailed fingering chart.

We wish you all the best as you continue to develop your musicianship, technique, and artistry!

~ Peter Boonshaft and Chris Bernotas

Margaret Donaghue is Professor of Clarinet and Director of the Woodwind Program at the Frost School of Music (University of Miami), and has performed as a soloist and chamber musician across three continents. She performs with PULSE Trio and MiamiClarinet, and is the Founder/Executive Director of the Blue Ridge Chamber Music Festival. She is heard frequently on Public Radio, as well as on multiple CD labels, and is a sought-after clinician and adjudicator. Dr. Donaghue is a Buffet Crampon Artist, as well as a D'Addario Woodwinds Artist.

alfred.com

Copyright © 2023 by Alfred Music
All rights reserved. Printed in USA.

ISBN-10: 1-4706-6653-7
ISBN-13: 978-1-4706-6653-8

Instrument photos provided courtesy of Jupiter Band Instruments/KHS America

Lesson 1

RESONANCE FINGERINGS (adding combinations of fingers from the right hand, as well as finger 2 and 3 of the left hand) can be used on G, A♭, A, and B♭ to improve tone and intonation. Experiment to see what sounds best on your instrument.

Examples of common resonance fingerings:

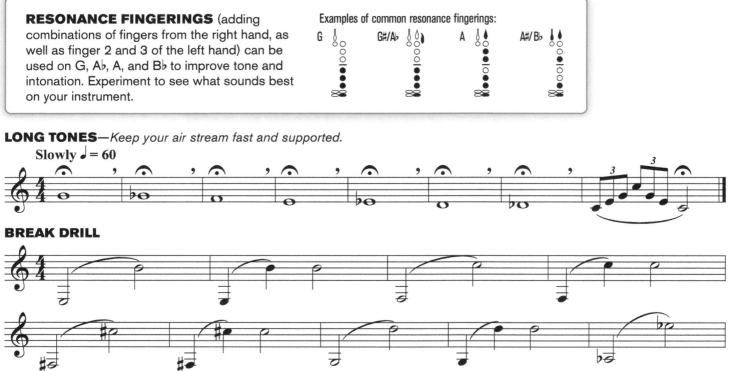

1 LONG TONES—*Keep your air stream fast and supported.*

Slowly ♩ = 60

2 BREAK DRILL

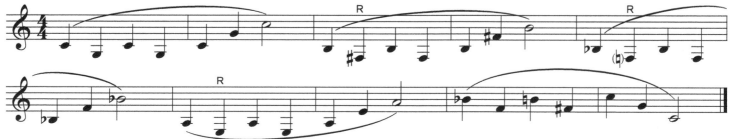

3 FLEXIBILITY—*For best technique, keep movement in one hand when possible. R indicates using the right pinky key for these notes.*

4 C MAJOR SCALE AND ARPEGGIO—*For all scale exercises that are written in octaves, practice each octave separately and then as a two octave scale and arpeggio.*

5 C MAJOR SCALE STUDY

Leave the right hand down

6 ARPEGGIO STUDY

7 ETUDE—*Proper hand position: Use the first knuckle of your first finger to open the A key. This allows a smooth crossing of the break. Play all etudes slowly with a steady tempo and good tone quality before speeding up. Always keep a good tone in mind and perform with musicality.*

8 ETUDE

9 ETUDE—*Resonance fingerings will improve the tone and intonation of throat tones. Experiment to see which fingering combinations work best for you. Practice this etude with two-bar phrases and then four-bar phrases.*

10 DUET—*For the most consistent articulation and tone in this range, keep the tongue position high and arched.*

Lesson 2

11 **CHALUMEAU DRILL**

Moderato ♩ = 102

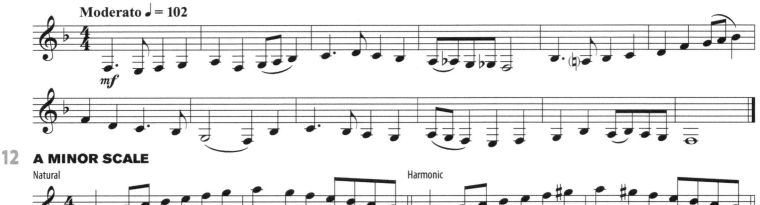

12 **A MINOR SCALE**

Natural   Harmonic

Melodic   Arpeggio

13 **A MINOR SCALE STUDY**—*Begin this exercise with right hand down.*

14 **ETUDE**

Moderately ♩ = 72

a tempo   *rall.*

15 **ETUDE**—*Subdivide for rhythmic accuracy on dotted, tied, and syncopated rhythms.*

Pensively ♩ = 60

16 PINKY DRILL—*Keep your pinkies rounded and relaxed. R indicates using the right pinky and L indicates the left pinky.*

17 CHROMATIC SCALE—*Use the alternate chromatic fingering for the F♯ and G♭ in this scale.*

18 CHROMATIC SCALE ETUDE—*Be sure to use alternate chromatic fingerings where appropriate.*

Moderately ♩ = 88

19 ETUDE—*After playing this etude as written, create or improvise a new ending for the last two measures.*

Lightly ♪ = 120

Lesson 3

20 **FLEXIBILITY**—*Remember to always have proper posture, embouchure, and hand position to promote performing with a beautiful tone.*

21 **CLARION DRILL**

22 **F MAJOR SCALE AND ARPEGGIO**—*Sing or hum these notes before playing them. Internalizing the pitch will help develop your aural skills.*

23 **F MAJOR SCALE STUDY**

24 **ETUDE**

Walking tempo ♩ = 104

25 ARPEGGIO STUDY

26 ETUDE

27 DUET

Lesson 4

28 **D MINOR SCALE**

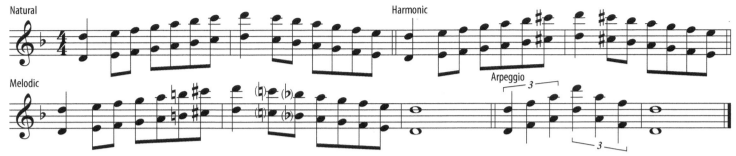

29 **D MINOR SCALE STUDY**

30 **ETUDE**

31 **ETUDE**

32 **DUET**—*Work toward matching each of the musical elements in this duet for a unified performance.*

Moderately ♩ = 100

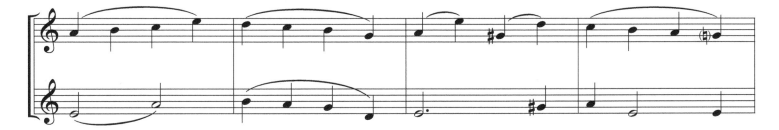

33 **ETUDE**—*Play this etude with an eighth-note pulse until the rhythm is accurate. Then, transition to the dotted-quarter-note pulse.*

Legato ♩. = 60

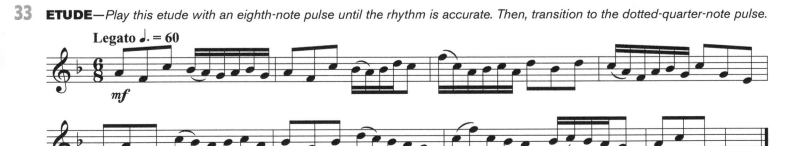

Lesson 5

34 **ETUDE**—*Trust your air support as you move into the altissimo register. Do not bite or squeeze to play the high D. Use the alternate chromatic fingering for the G♭ in measure 12.*

35 **ETUDE**

36 **ETUDE**

37 ETUDE

Stately ♩ = 98

38 DUET

Maestoso ♩ = 72

39 ETUDE

Cantabile ♩ = 72

12

Lesson 6

40 **FLEXIBILITY**

41 **G MAJOR SCALE AND ARPEGGIO**

42 **G MAJOR SCALE STUDY**—*Using manuscript paper or notation software, compose a new scale study that you think is even more challenging.*

43 **RANGE EXTENSION**—*Remember to add your pinky on the A♭/E♭ key for all altissimo notes above C♯.*

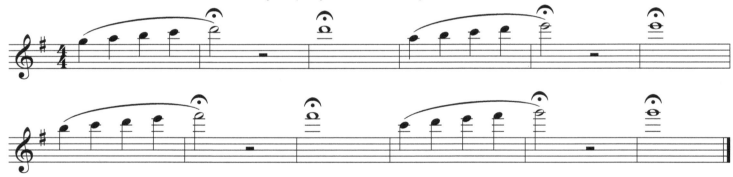

44 **RANGE EXTENSION**

45 **INTERVAL STUDY**—*Once you are comfortable with this as written, practice it an octave higher.*

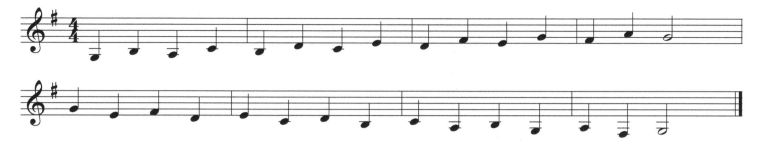

46 **ETUDE**

Andantino ♩ = 80

47 **ETUDE**—*Maintain air support as you move through dynamic changes. Practice this etude with two-bar phrases and then four-bar phrases.*

Dolce ♩ = 80

48 **ETUDE**

Moderately ♩ = 112

Lesson 7

49 **FLEXIBILITY**

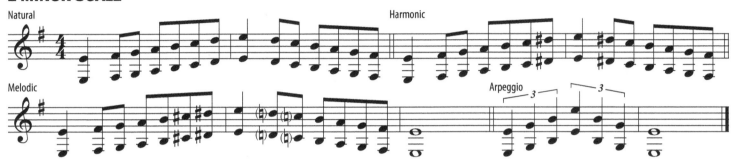

50 **E MINOR SCALE**

Natural   Harmonic

Melodic   Arpeggio

51 **E MINOR SCALE STUDY**

52 **ETUDE**

Majestically ♩ = 88

53 **ALTISSIMO DRILL**—*When playing in the upper register, use your air support, keep the tongue position high and arched, and don't bite.*

Very slowly ♩ = 40

54 ETUDE

55 ETUDE—*After successfully playing this etude, seek guidance from a teacher for ways you can refine your performance.*

56 ETUDE

Lesson 8

57 FLEXIBILITY—*Keep your fingers rounded and relaxed.*

58 B♭ MAJOR SCALE AND ARPEGGIO

59 B♭ MAJOR SCALE STUDY

Moderately ♩ = 112

60 ETUDE—*If this exercise is not rhythmically even at the dotted-quarter-note pulse, try setting your metronome to the eighth-note pulse of ♪ = 180. Use a light, relaxed, legato tongue.*

Adagio ♩. = 60

61 ETUDE—*Be creative with the musicality of this etude by altering and adding your own dynamic markings.*

Cantabile ♩ = 72

62 DUET

63 G MINOR SCALE

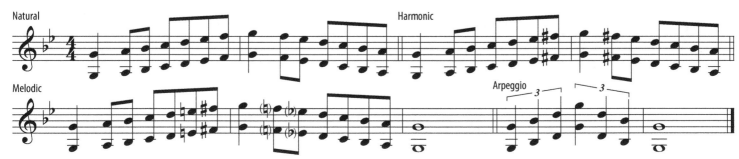

64 G MINOR SCALE STUDY

65 ETUDE

Lesson 9

GRACE NOTES are ornaments that are performed before the beat or on the beat, depending on the musical time period, style, context, and notation. The last example below shows how unslashed grace notes would be performed in the Classical period. Listen to music from various historical periods and notice the different approaches to the performance of grace notes.

Most often performed before the beat

Classical period, no slash. On the beat (in time).

66 GRACE NOTES—*Play these grace notes just before the main note.*

67 ETUDE

68 ETUDE—*An appoggiatura is a grace note without a slash that is played on the beat. In this exercise, measures 1 and 5, as well as measures 3 and 7, would be played the same.*

69 ETUDE

70 ETUDE

71 ETUDE

72 ETUDE—*Record your performance of this etude. Recognize the personal musical growth you have made from when you sight-read the piece. Think about the technical and musical ways your performance has improved. Do you hear a difference?*

73 ETUDE

Lesson 10

74 **LONG TONES**—*For best intonation, the "speed" of the air stream remains fast throughout dynamics changes; the "amount" of air is what changes.*

75 **FLEXIBILITY**

76 **ETUDE**

77 **ETUDE**

78 CHROMATIC SCALE

79 CHROMATIC RANGE

80 MAJOR SCALE RANGE

81 DUET

Andante ♩ = 108

22

Lesson 11

82 FLEXIBILITY

* Use this fingering:

83 D MAJOR SCALE AND ARPEGGIO

84 D MAJOR SCALE STUDY

Moderately ♩ = 120

85 ETUDE

Adagio ♩ = 60

86 ETUDE—*Keep the tongue relaxed throughout. Move the tongue as little as possible, staying close to the reed.*

Allegro ♩ = 90

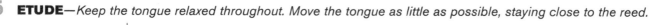

continued on
next page

87 ETUDE

Andante ♩ = 100

88 ETUDE—*After performing this etude, discuss the various elements of the musical work with a peer or teacher.*

Moderato ♩ = 88

89 ETUDE

Briskly ♩. = 80

24

Lesson 12

90 FLEXIBILITY

91 B MINOR SCALE

92 B MINOR SCALE STUDY

93 B MINOR SCALE STUDY

94 DUET

A **TRILL** is an ornament that is performed by alternating rapidly between the written note and the next diatonic note above. Sometimes you will see a natural, sharp, or flat sign with a trill, which means to alternate between the written note and the next altered note. Always check the key signature. Find various options of trill fingerings online.

95 **TRILLS**—*Use your metronome to ensure an even and consistent rhythm.*

Evenly ♩ = 72

96 **TRILLS**—*Practice this exercise to ensure your trills are played evenly. Once you are comfortable with this exercise as written, try playing it in cut time (𝅗𝅥=160). For the F to G trill: Finger F, trill the G♯ key. For the B♭ to C: Finger B♭, trill the top 2 side keys.*

Presto ♩ = 160

97 **TRILLS**—*Practice measures 1–5 at a slow tempo to reinforce muscle memory, gradually increasing the tempo. This exercise will help ensure that your trills are played evenly.*

Presto ♩ = 160

98 **ETUDE**—*Depending on the style or historical context, a trill may start with an upper neighbor as shown here. Practice these trills with and without the upper neighbor. Also, grace notes are often used at the end of a trill. This ornament is also known as a nachschläge. For the A to B trill: Finger A, trill the top side key*

Moderately ♩ = 90

Lesson 13

99 FLEXIBILITY

100 E♭ MAJOR SCALE AND ARPEGGIO

101 E♭ MAJOR SCALE STUDY

102 ETUDE

103 ETUDE

104 **DUET**

28

Lesson 14

105 LONG TONES

Slowly ♩ = 60

106 FLEXIBILITY

107 C MINOR SCALE

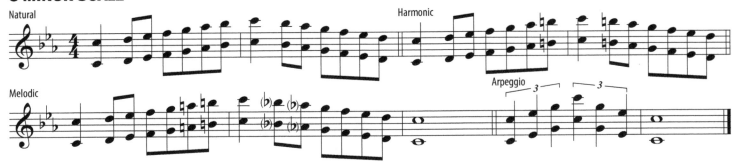

108 C MINOR SCALE STUDY

Moderately ♩ = 100

109 ETUDE

Larghetto ♩ = 60

110 DUET

111 ETUDE

* Use this fingering:

112 DUET—*While playing duets, both performers must listen critically to evaluate and adjust intonation. For the Bb in this duet, try using the third finger of each hand and the low F key (Bb resonance fingering).*

Lesson 15

113 FLEXIBILITY

114 A MAJOR SCALE AND ARPEGGIO

115 A MAJOR SCALE STUDY

116 ETUDE

117 ETUDE

118 **LONG TONES**

Slowly ♩ = 60

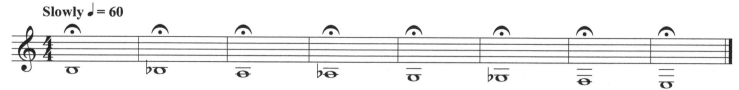

119 **F♯ MINOR SCALE**

120 **F♯ MINOR SCALE STUDY**

Andante ♩ = 88

121 **ETUDE**

Moderato ♩ = 120

Lesson 16

122 **DUET**—*When playing ♪♪, remember to think of a sixteenth-note subdivision.*

123 **ETUDE**

124 **DUET**—*What musical elements in this duet make it engaging? How does the form contribute to the musical work?*

125 **ETUDE**

Lesson 17

126 FLEXIBILITY

127 Ab MAJOR SCALE AND ARPEGGIO

> A **TURN** or **GRUPPETTO** is an ornament that involves playing the written note, followed by the note above it, returning to the original note, then playing the note below it, and finally ending on the original note.

128 Ab MAJOR SCALE STUDY

Adagio ♩ = 72

mf

129 Ab MAJOR SCALE STUDY

Moderato ♩ = 112

Slide if necessary

mf

Slide if necessary

R

130 ETUDE

Andante ♩ = 80

mf

continued on next page

131 F MINOR SCALE

132 F MINOR SCALE STUDY

133 ETUDE

Lesson 18

134 LONG TONES

Slowly ♩ = 60

135 FLEXIBILITY

136 E MAJOR SCALE AND ARPEGGIO

137 E MAJOR SCALE STUDY

Moderately ♩ = 100

138 ETUDE

Andante ♩ = 108

139 ETUDE

Adagio ♩. = 60

140 C♯ MINOR SCALES

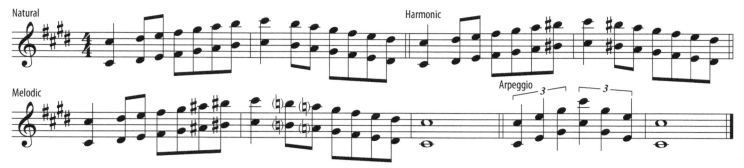

Natural — Harmonic

Melodic — Arpeggio

141 C♯ MINOR SCALE STUDY

Moderato ♩ = 108
mf

142 ETUDE

Allegro ♩ = 120
mf

143 DUET

Adagio ♩ = 66
mf
mf

Lesson 19

144 **FLEXIBILITY**

145 **ETUDE**

146 **ETUDE**

147 **ETUDE**

148 **DUET**

149 **ETUDE**

150 **DUET**—*Use critical listening to improve the performance of all musical elements in this duet.*

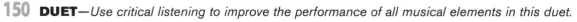

Lesson 20

151 ETUDE

Moderato ♩ = 88

152 DUET

Moderato ♩ = 108

153 ETUDE

Adagio ♩. = 80

154 ETUDE

155 DUET

156 ETUDE

42

157 **ETUDE**

Fanfare ♩ = 120

158 **ETUDE**

Majestic ♩ = 100

159 **DUET**

Majestic ♩ = 108

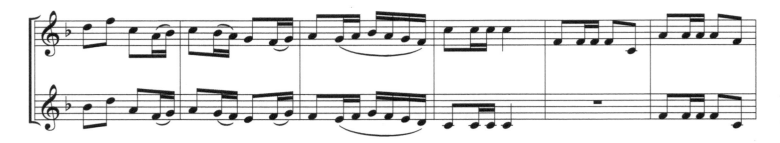

Lesson 21

160 FLEXIBILITY

161 D♭ MAJOR SCALE AND ARPEGGIO

162 ETUDE—*Use side G♭ where appropriate.*

163 ETUDE

164 B♭ MINOR SCALES

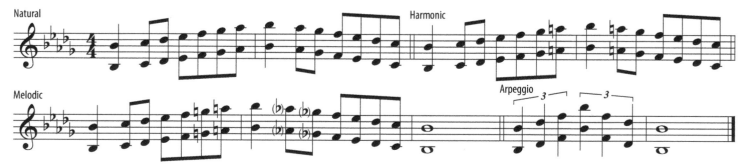

165 ETUDE

Lesson 22

166 **LONG TONES**

Slowly ♩ = 60

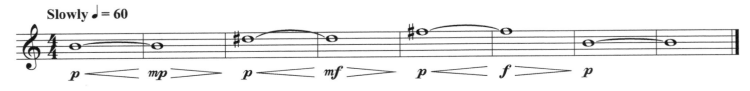

167 **B MAJOR SCALE AND ARPEGGIO**

168 **ETUDE**

Andante ♩ = 80

169 **ETUDE**

Adagio ♩ = 72

170 **A♭ MINOR SCALE** *(enharmonic spelling of G♯ minor)*

Natural · Harmonic · Melodic · Arpeggio

171 **ETUDE**

Adagio ♩ = 66

Major Scales

C MAJOR

F MAJOR

B♭ MAJOR

E♭ MAJOR

A♭ MAJOR

D♭ MAJOR

G♭ MAJOR

C♭ MAJOR

G MAJOR

D MAJOR

A MAJOR

E MAJOR

B MAJOR

F♯ MAJOR

C♯ MAJOR

Minor Scales

A MINOR

Natural Harmonic Melodic

D MINOR

Natural Harmonic Melodic

G MINOR

Natural Harmonic Melodic

C MINOR

Natural Harmonic Melodic

F MINOR

B♭ MINOR

E♭ MINOR

A♭ MINOR

E MINOR

B MINOR

F♯ MINOR

C♯ MINOR

G♯ MINOR

D♯ MINOR

A♯ MINOR

Clarinet Fingering Chart

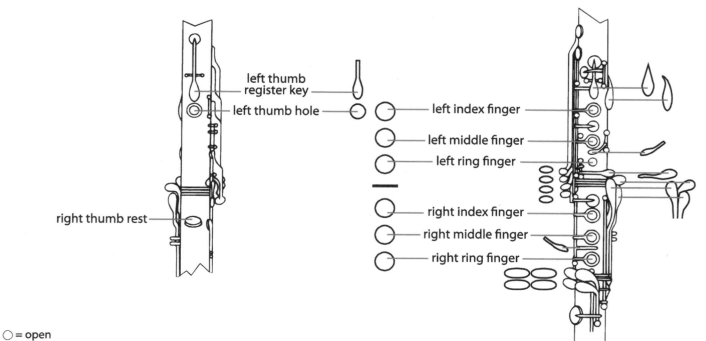

◯ = open
● = pressed down

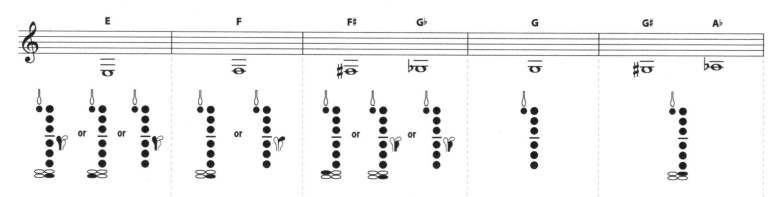

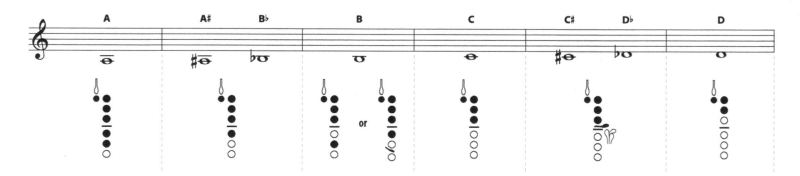

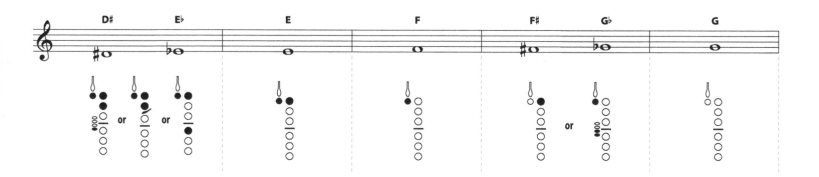

48

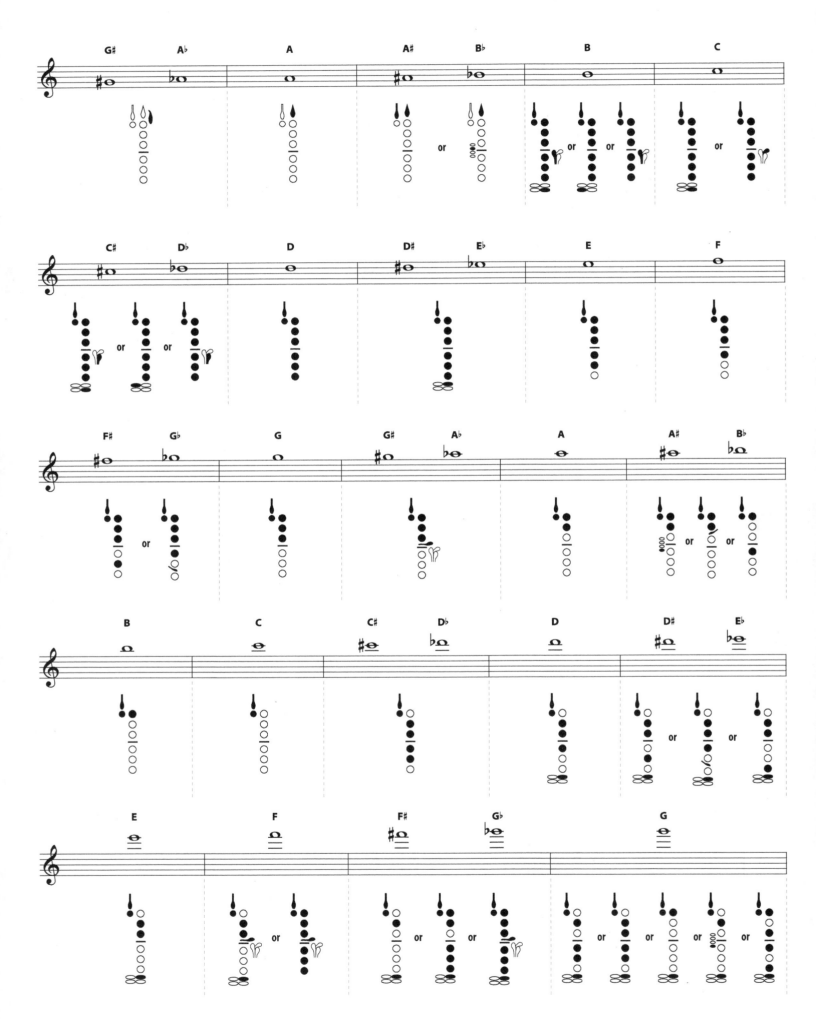